D1711381

To:

_____

From:

_____

© 2011 by Barbour Publishing, Inc.

ISBN 978-1-61626-449-9

Scripture quotations marked KJV are taken from the King James Version of the Bible.

Scripture quotations marked NIV are taken from the HOLY BIBLE, NEW INTERNATIONAL VERSION®. NIV®. Copyright © 1973, 1978, 1984, 2010 by Biblica, Inc.™ Used by permission. All rights reserved worldwide.

Scripture quotations marked MSG are from THE MESSAGE. Copyright © by Eugene H. Peterson 1993, 1994, 1995, 1996, 2000, 2001, 2002. Used by permission of NavPress Publishing Group.

Scripture quotations marked NLT are taken from the Holy Bible, New Living Translation, copyright © 1996, 2004. Used by permission of Tyndale House Publishers, Inc. Wheaton, Illinois 60189, U.S.A. All rights reserved.

Scripture quotations marked NRSV are taken from the New Revised Standard Version Bible, copyright 1989, Division of Christian Education of the National Council of the Churches of Christ in the United States of America. Used by permission. All rights reserved.

Cover and Interior Design: Thinkpen Design, Inc., www.thinkpendesign.com

Published by Barbour Publishing, Inc., P.O. Box 719, Uhrichsville, Ohio 44683, www.barbourbooks.com

Our mission is to publish and distribute inspirational products offering exceptional value and biblical encouragement to the masses.

 Member of the
Evangelical Christian
Publishers Association

Printed in China.

NATURE'S PRAISE

Classics

Music and Inspiration to Celebrate the Outdoors

BARBOUR
PUBLISHING

Every moment is full of wonder,

and God is always present.

Keep your face
upturned to [God]
as the flowers
do to the sun.
Look, and your soul
shall live and grow.

H ANNAH W HITALL S MITH

Never lose an opportunity of
seeing anything that is beautiful,
for beauty is God's handwriting—
a wayside sacrament.
Welcome it in every fair sky,
in every fair flower,
and thank God for
it as a cup of blessing.

RALPH WALDO EMERSON

I believe that in each little thing created by God, there is more than what is understood, even if it is a little ant.

TERESA OF AVILA

Whatsoever things are lovely. . .

think on these things.

PHILIPPIANS 4:8 KJV

As we grow in our capacities
to discover the joys that God
has placed in our lives,
life becomes a glorious
experience of discovering
His endless wonders.

UNKNOWN

It's not what you look at that
matters, it's what you see.

HENRY DAVID THOREAU

I'll tell you how the sun rose—
one ribbon at a time.

EMILY DICKINSON

Earth with her thousand voices, praises God.

Samuel Taylor Coleridge

For you make me glad by your deeds, Lord; I sing for joy at what your hands have done.

When you take a flower in your
hand and really look at it,
it's your world for a moment. . . .

GEORGIA O'KEEFE

The human spirit needs places
where nature has not been
arranged by the hand of man.

UNKNOWN

A simple pleasure, like a butterfly
on the wing, inspires our spirits
to soar toward the Creator
of such intricate beauty.

JOANIE GARBORG

Teach me the art of creating

islands of stillness,

in which I can absorb the beauty

of everyday things:

clouds, trees, a snatch of music. . . .

MARION STROUD

You're my place of quiet retreat;
I wait for your Word to renew me. . . .
Therefore I lovingly embrace
everything you say.

Psalm 119:114, 119 msg

Have you ever observed
a hummingbird moving
about in an aerial dance
among the flowers—
a living prismatic gem. . . .
It is a creature of
such fairylike loveliness as
to mock all description.

W. H. HUDSON

I once had a sparrow alight
upon my shoulder for a
moment while I was hoeing
in a village garden, and I felt
that I was more distinguished
by that circumstance than
I should have been by any
epaulet I could have worn.

HENRY DAVID THOREAU

There are two ways to
live your life. One is as
though nothing is a miracle.
The other is as though
everything is a miracle.

ALBERT EINSTEIN

If the day and the
night are such that you greet
them with joy, and life emits
a fragrance like flowers
and sweet-scented herbs,
is more elastic, more starry,
more immortal—that is your success.

HENRY DAVID THOREAU

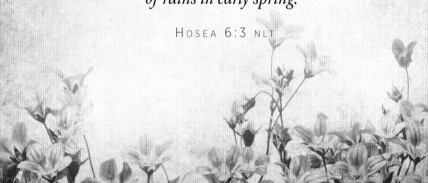

"Oh, that we might know the
LORD! Let us press on to know him.
He will respond to us surely as the
arrival of dawn or the coming
of rains in early spring."

HOSEA 6:3 NLT

Truly it may
be said that
the outside of a
mountain is good
for the inside
of a man.

GEORGE WHERRY

I've always regarded nature
as the clothing of God.

ALAN HOVHANESS

Give me. . .at sunrise a garden
of beautiful flowers where
I can walk undisturbed.

WALT WHITMAN

Always begin anew with the day, just as nature does; it is one of the sensible things that nature does.

GEORGE E. WOODBERRY

Be still, and know that I am God.

PSALM 46:10 NIV

Blue skies with white clouds
on summer days. A myriad of
stars on clear moonlit nights.
Tulips and roses and violets
and dandelions and daisies.
Bluebirds and laughter and
sunshine and Easter.
See how [God] loves us!

ALICE CHAPIN

Happiness is as a butterfly,
which, when pursued, is always
beyond our grasp, but which,
if you will sit down quietly,
may alight upon you.

NATHANIEL HAWTHORNE

The key to happiness belongs

to everyone on earth who

recognizes simple things

as treasures of great worth.

Unknown

Any man that walks the mead

In bud, or blade,

or bloom, may find

A meaning suited to his mind.

ALFRED TENNYSON

He fills my life with good things.

Psalm 103:5 nlt

The God who holds the
whole world in His hands
wraps Himself in the splendor
of the sun's light and walks
among the clouds.

UNKNOWN

All things bright and beautiful,

all creatures great and small,

all things wise and wonderful,

the Lord God made them all.

Cecil Frances Alexander

I think that if ever a mortal heard the voice of God, it would be in a garden at the cool of the day.

F. FRANKFORT MOORE

It is not so much for its
beauty that the forest makes
a claim upon men's hearts,
as for that subtle something,
that quality of air,
that emanation from old trees,
that so wonderfully changes
and renews a weary spirit.

ROBERT LOUIS STEVENSON

Yes, my soul, find rest in God;

my hope comes from him.

Psalm 62:5 niv

You must not know too much,

or be too precise or scientific

about birds and trees and

flowers and watercraft;

a certain free margin,

and even vagueness. . .

helps your enjoyment

of these things.

WALT WHITMAN

Hope is like the sun, which,

as we journey toward it,

casts the shadow of our

burden behind us.

SAMUEL SMILES

The sun. . .in its full glory,

either at rising or setting—

this and many other like

blessings we enjoy daily;

and for the most of them,

because they are so common,

most men forget to pay their praises.

But let us not.

Izaak Walton

How can one help shivering with
delight when one's hot fingers
close around the stem of a live
flower, cool from the shade
and stiff with newborn vigor!

COLETTE

Come near to God and he will

come near to you.

JAMES 4:8 NIV

This is my Father's world:
I rest me in the thought
Of rocks and trees,
Of skies and seas;
His hand the wonders wrought.

Maltbie D. Babcock

All are but parts
of one stupendous
whole, whose body
nature is,
and God the soul.

ALEXANDER POPE

I often think flowers are the
angels' alphabet whereby
they write on hills and fields
mysterious and beautiful lessons
for us to feel and learn.

LOUISA MAY ALCOTT

Seeing our Father in everything
makes life one long thanksgiving
and gives a rest of heart.

HANNAH WHITALL SMITH

[God] refreshes my soul.

PSALM 23:3 NIV

Now I see the secret of
making the best person:
it is to grow in the open air
and to eat and sleep
with the earth.

WALT WHITMAN

Everyone must take time to sit
and watch the leaves turn.

ELIZABETH LAWRENCE

I thank You, God,

for this most amazing day,

for the leaping greenly spirits of

trees, and for the blue dream

of sky and for everything

which is natural, which is

infinite, which is yes.

E. E. CUMMINGS

Our Creator would never have
made such lovely days,
and have given us the deep hearts
to enjoy them, above and beyond
all thought, unless we were
meant to be immortal.

NATHANIEL HAWTHORNE

My soul will rejoice in the Lord.

PSALM 35:9 NIV

To one who has been long
in city pent, 'tis very sweet
to look into the fair
and open face of heaven,
to breathe a prayer
full in the smile of the
blue firmament.

JOHN KEATS

See how nature—trees,
flowers, grass—grows in silence;
see the stars, the moon,
and the sun, how they move in
silence. . . . We need silence
to be able to touch souls.

MOTHER TERESA

One touch of nature makes the whole world kin.

WILLIAM SHAKESPEARE

No site in the forest is
without significance, not a glade,
not a thicket that does not provide
analogies to the labyrinth of human
thoughts. Who among those people
with a cultivated spirit, or whose heart
has been wounded, can walk in a forest
without the forest speaking to him?

HONORÉ DE BALZAC

*"Come to me, all you that are weary
and are carrying heavy burdens,
and I will give you rest."*

MATTHEW 11:28 NRSV

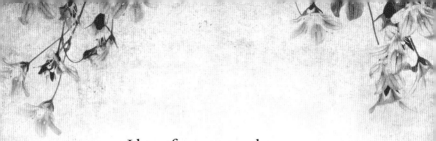

I long for scenes where
man has never trod;
A place where woman never
smil'd or wept;
There to abide with my creator,
God. . . .

JOHN CLARE

A thing of beauty
is a joy forever:
its loveliness
increases; it will
never pass into
nothingness.

JOHN KEATS

A morning glory at my window

satisfies me more than

the metaphysics of books.

WALT WHITMAN

Climb the mountains and get
their good tidings.
Nature's peace will flow into you
as sunshine flows into trees.
The winds will blow their own
freshness into you,
and the storms their energy,
while cares will drop off
like autumn leaves.

JOHN MUIR

If I go up to the heavens,

you are there; if I make my bed

in the depths, you are there.

If I rise on wings of the dawn,

if I settle on the far side of the sea,

even there your hand will guide me,

your right hand will hold me fast.

PSALM 139:8–10 NIV

All that is good, all that is true,
all that is beautiful, all that is
beneficent, be it great or small,
be it perfect or fragmentary,
natural as well as supernatural,
moral as well as material,
comes from God.

JOHN NEWMAN

Joy, all creatures drink at nature's bosoms. . .

FRIEDRICH VON SCHILLER

Flowers. . .are a proud assertion
that a ray of beauty outvalues all
the utilities of the world.

RALPH WALDO EMERSON

There is springtime
in my soul today,
For, when the Lord is near,
The dove of peace sings in my heart,
The flowers of grace appear.

ELIZA HEWITT

The steadfast love of the Lord never ceases, his mercies never come to an end; they are new every morning; great is your faithfulness.

LAMENTATIONS 3:22–23 NRSV

In all ranks of life the human heart
yearns for the beautiful;
and the beautiful things that
God makes are His gift to all alike.

Harriet Beecher Stowe

The sky is the daily bread

of the eyes.

RALPH WALDO EMERSON

Art gallery? Who needs it?
Look up at the swirling silver-lined
clouds in the magnificent sky
or at the silently blazing stars at
midnight. How could indoor art be
any more masterfully created than
God's museum of nature?

GREY LIVINGSTON

I wear a coat of angels'
breath and warm myself
in [God's] love.

EMME WOODULL-BACHE

I lift up my eyes to the mountains—

where does my help come from?

*My help comes from the L*ORD*,*

the Maker of heaven and earth.

PSALM 121:1–2 NIV

Ordinary things have a great
power to reveal the mysterious
nearness of a caring,
liberated God. . . . In what seems
ordinary and everyday,
there is always more than
at first meets the eye.

CHARLES CUMMINGS

Between the house and the
store there are little pockets of
happiness. A bird, a garden,
a friend's greeting, a child's smile,
a cat in the sunshine needing a
stroke. Recognize them or ignore
them. It's always up to you.

PAM BROWN

Where others see
but the dawn
coming over the
hill, I see the soul
of God shouting
for joy.

WILLIAM BLAKE

The more I study nature,

the more I am amazed

at the Creator.

LOUIS PASTEUR

Surely your goodness and love will
follow me all the days of my life,
and I will dwell in the house
of the L ORD *forever.*

P SALM 23:6 NIV

Nature. . .unfolds her treasures
to [man's] search,
unseals his eye, illumes his mind,
and purifies his heart;
and influence breathes from all the
sights and sounds of her existence.

ALFRED BILLINGS STREET

All I want is to stand in a field and to smell green, to taste the air, to feel the earth. . .

PHILLIP PULFREY

Plant kindness and gather love.

UNKNOWN

The wonder of living
is held within the beauty
of silence, the glory of sunlight,
the sweetness of fresh spring air,
the quiet strength of earth,
and the love that lies at the
very root of all things.

UNKNOWN

Let the rivers clap their hands,

let the mountains sing

together for joy.

The year's at the
spring and day's
at the morn. . . .
God's in His
heaven—all's right
with the world!

ROBERT BROWNING